NORTH CAROLINA

The Old North State

BY
JOHN HAMILTON

&

Abdo & Daughters

An imprint of Abdo Publishing | abdopublishing.com

abdopublishing.com

Published by ABDO Publishing, a division of ABDO, PO Box 398166, Minneapolis, Minnesota 55439. Copyright © 2017 by Abdo Consulting Group, Inc. International copyrights reserved in all countries. No part of this book may be reproduced in any form without written permission from the publisher. ABDO & Daughters™ is a trademark and logo of ABDO Publishing.

Printed in the United States of America, North Mankato, Minnesota.
052016
092016

Editor: Sue Hamilton   **Contributing Editor:** Bridget O'Brien
Graphic Design: Sue Hamilton
Cover Art Direction: Candice Keimig   **Cover Photo Selection:** Neil Klinepier
Cover Photo: iStock
Interior Images: Alamy, AP, Architect of the Capitol-Washington, DC, British Museum-John White, Carolina Hurricanes, Carolina Panthers, Charlotte Hornets, Country Music Hall of Fame and Museum, Dreamstime, Duke Blue Devils, George P.A. Healy, Getty, Gilbert Stewart, Granger Collection, History in Full Color-Restoration/Colorization, Indiana.gov, iStock, John Hamilton, Library of Congress, Mike Kight, Mile High Maps, New York Public Library, One Mile Up, Minden Pictures, North Carolina State University, NC State Wolfpack, University of North Carolina Tar Heels, Wake Forest Demon Deacons, & Wikimedia.

Statistics: *State and City Populations*, U.S. Census Bureau, July 1, 2015/2014 estimates; *Land and Water Area*, U.S. Census Bureau, 2010 Census, MAF/TIGER database; *State Temperature Extremes*, NOAA National Climatic Data Center; *Climatology and Average Annual Precipitation*, NOAA National Climatic Data Center, 1980-2015 statewide averages; *State Highest and Lowest Points*, NOAA National Geodetic Survey.

Websites: To learn more about the United States, visit booklinks.abdopublishing.com. These links are routinely monitored and updated to provide the most current information available.

Cataloging-in-Publication Data

Names: Hamilton, John, 1959- author.
Title: North Carolina / by John Hamilton.
Description: Minneapolis, MN : Abdo Publishing, [2017] | Series: The United
    States of America | Includes index.
Identifiers: LCCN 2015957716 | ISBN 9781680783353 (lib. bdg.) |
    ISBN 9781680774399 (ebook)
Subjects: LCSH: North Carolina--Juvenile literature.
Classification: DDC 975.6--dc23
LC record available at http://lccn.loc.gov/2015957716

CONTENTS

THE OLD NORTH STATE

North Carolina is a mix of old and new. It has unmistakable Southern roots. Its people are friendly and polite, and they share a love of BBQ cooking, basketball, and slow meanders through Appalachian Mountain forests. But the modern world has come full force to North Carolina. In its central Piedmont region, new computer and biotech companies, plus many acclaimed universities, have transformed the state into a high-tech powerhouse. It is one of the fastest-growing states in the nation.

In 1629, England's King Charles I created an American colony called the Province of Carolina. It was much larger than today's North Carolina. It also covered the lands of modern South Carolina, Georgia, and several other Southern states. In 1729, the colony was officially divided. The southern lands were called South Carolina, while the older, northern settlements were called North Carolina. That is why today it is nicknamed "The Old North State."

The 1903 first flight of a heavier-than-air aircraft by the Wright brothers is remembered in Kill Devil Hills, North Carolina.

Completed in 1870, the
Cape Hatteras Lighthouse is
the tallest brick lighthouse
in America. It is 198 feet
(60 m) tall, has 269 steps,
and its light can be seen for
more than 28 miles (45 km).

QUICK FACTS

Name: North Carolina is named after England's King Charles I (1600-1649). The word Carolina is a form of the word Carolus, which is a way of writing Charles in Latin.

State Capital: Raleigh, population 439,896

Date of Statehood: November 21, 1789 (12th state)

Population: 10,042,802 (9th-most populous state)

Area (Total Land and Water): 53,819 square miles (139,391 sq km), 28th-largest state

Largest City: Charlotte, population 809,958

Nicknames: The Old North State; The Tar Heel State

Motto: *Esse quam videri* (To be, rather than to seem)

State Bird: Cardinal

State Flower: Dogwood

State Rock: Granite

State Tree: Pine

State Song: "The Old North State"

Highest Point: Mount Mitchell, 6,684 feet (2,037 m)

Lowest Point: Atlantic Ocean, 0 feet (0 m)

Mount Mitchell

Average July High Temperature: 88°F (31°C)

Record High Temperature: 110°F (43°C), in Fayetteville on August 21, 1983

Atlantic Ocean

Average January Low Temperature: 29°F (-2°C)

Record Low Temperature: -34°F (-37°C), on Mount Mitchell on January 21, 1985

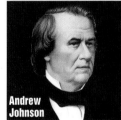

Andrew Johnson

Average Annual Precipitation: 49 inches (124 cm)

Number of U.S. Senators: 2

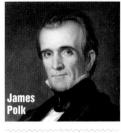

James Polk

Number of U.S. Representatives: 13

U.S. Presidents Born in North Carolina: Andrew Johnson (1808-1875); James Polk (1795-1849)

U.S. Postal Service Abbreviation: NC

QUICK FACTS

GEOGRAPHY

North Carolina is in the South Atlantic States region of the United States. It borders the Atlantic Ocean to the east. To the north is the state of Virginia. Its neighbor to the west is Tennessee. To the south are Georgia and South Carolina. North Carolina covers 53,819 square miles (139,391 sq km). That makes it the 28th-largest state in the country.

North Carolina has three geographic regions. Rising from east to west, they include the Coastal Plain, the Piedmont, and the Appalachian Mountains.

The Coastal Plain is a flat, low-lying area next to the Atlantic Ocean. It extends almost to the middle of the state. Near the shore, there are many marshes and swamps. The Great Dismal Swamp once covered 2,000 square miles (5,180 sq km). Today, 175 square miles (453 sq km) are preserved as the Great Dismal Swamp National Wildlife Refuge.

Great Dismal Swamp

North Carolina's total land and water area
is 53,819 square miles (139,391 sq km).
It is the 28th-largest state. The state capital
is Raleigh.

GEOGRAPHY

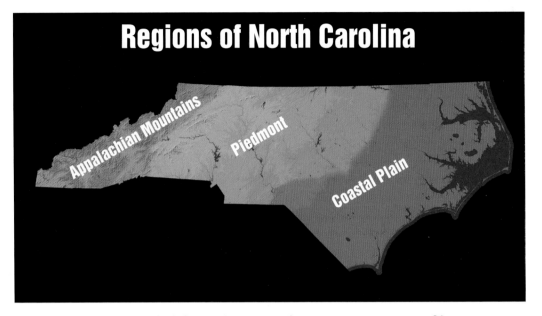

Regions of North Carolina

Appalachian Mountains

Piedmont

Coastal Plain

The coast is shielded from the ocean by a narrow group of barrier islands called the Outer Banks. They lie as far as 30 miles (48 km) off the mainland. The chain of narrow, sandy islands is more than 175 miles (282 km) long, but only 15 to 30 miles (24 to 48 km) wide.

The Piedmont is a region in central North Carolina. It covers about one-third of the state. The boundary between the Piedmont and Coastal Plain region is called the fall line, or fall zone. It is where the hard bedrock of the Piedmont meets the softer eastern rocks. The ground descends steeply. The zone is easy to spot when following rivers. At the fall line, there are many natural waterfalls and rapids.

Looking Glass Falls is one of many waterfalls in North Carolina's Appalachian Mountain region.

The Piedmont consists of gently rolling hills. Early textile mills and gristmills harnessed the power of swiftly moving streams and rivers. Today, most of North Carolina's major cities are in this region.

The Appalachian Mountain region is in the far western part of North Carolina. There are several smaller ranges, called sub-ranges, within the Appalachians. The two main sub-ranges include the Blue Ridge and Great Smoky Mountains. The state's highest point is Mount Mitchell. Rising to 6,684 feet (2,037 m), it is the tallest mountain east of the Mississippi River.

Important rivers in North Carolina include the Roanoke, Tar, Neuse, Cape Fear, Yadkin, Catawba, and French Broad Rivers. The largest natural lake in the state is Lake Mattamuskeet.

Lake Mattamuskeet, North Carolina's largest natural lake, lies just inside the state's northeastern coastline. The lake is shallow, usually only 2 to 3 feet (.6 to .9 m) deep.

CLIMATE AND
WEATHER

North Carolina's climate varies because of its different regions. There are four distinct seasons. Overall, temperatures are usually mild, thanks to the state's southern location.

The Coastal Plain region is warmed by air blowing from the Atlantic Ocean. That causes mild winter temperatures. Summers are moderately warm, but the humidity can be high.

The Piedmont region is too far inland to be affected much by ocean breezes. Winters are colder, and summers hotter, than on the Coastal Plain.

A mister cools people off during a July street festival in Asheville, North Carolina.

North Carolina's coast may experience high winds and heavy rains from tropical storms and hurricanes. Hurricane Arthur hit North Carolina in 2014.

In far western North Carolina, the Appalachian Mountains are the coldest part of the state, thanks to high altitudes. Temperatures in winter are very cold, while summers are cool. The coldest temperature ever recorded in North Carolina occurred on Mount Mitchell, the state's highest point. On January 21, 1985, the thermometer plunged to -34°F (-37°C).

North Carolina gets plenty of rain throughout the year. The average yearly precipitation statewide is 49 inches (124 cm). It is driest in the autumn. The eastern slopes of the Appalachian Mountains commonly receive 90 inches (229 cm) of rain and snow yearly. Summer thunderstorms sometimes bring severe weather, including tornadoes. Hurricanes strike North Carolina about once every 10 years on average.

CLIMATE AND WEATHER

PLANTS AND
ANIMALS

Each of North Carolina's three regions is home to many kinds of plants and animals. About 60 percent of the state is covered with forests. Overall, North Carolina has more than 4,000 plant species.

The official state tree is the pine. Many types of this common tree grow throughout North Carolina. It is very important to the state's history. One of North Carolina's nicknames is "The Tar Heel State." In the days of sailing ships, the state's vast pine forests were heavily logged. They were processed to make sticky tar, resin, and turpentine, crucial ingredients in constructing ships.

A deciduous forest in autumn in North Carolina's Blue Ridge Mountains.

In the marshes of the Coastal Plain region are cordgrass, cattails, saw grass, and carnivorous Venus flytraps. Sea oats grow on the sandy

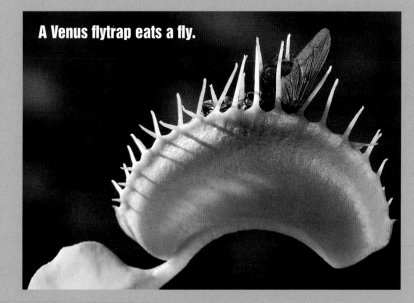

A Venus flytrap eats a fly.

dunes of the Outer Banks. Trees growing on the mainland include palmettos, cypress, oak, and sweet gum.

Many kinds of trees grow in the Piedmont region. The most common include pine, oak, poplar, and hickory trees.

In the lower elevations of the Appalachian Mountains are deciduous forests of sugar maple, yellow birch, beech, dogwood, and many others. In the highest parts of the mountains are spruce and fir trees.

Sea Oats

There are more than 1,200 species of mammals, birds, reptiles, and fish in North Carolina. Black bears are found in the Coastal Plain wetlands, as well as the Appalachian Mountains. North Carolina's most familiar forest animal is the white-tailed deer. Other common animals include rabbits, raccoons, opossums, bobcats, coyotes, red foxes, beavers, minks, muskrats, and striped skunks. The official state animal is the gray squirrel.

Dozens of species of birds can be found in the skies of North Carolina. They include mourning doves, bobwhites, quails, canvasback ducks, chickadees, great horned owls, herons, woodpeckers, wrens, and wild turkeys. The cardinal is North Carolina's state bird. The male has a bright-red coloring and a loud, whistling song.

Black Bear

American alligators live in North Carolina's freshwater swamps and lakes. They eat fish, wading birds, snakes, frogs, turtles, and small mammals.

Swimming in North Carolina's many rivers, lakes, and wetlands are brook and rainbow trout, bass, perch, bluegill, pickerel, sunfish, and catfish. The official state freshwater fish is the Southern Appalachian brook trout. It is sometimes called speckled trout because of its speckled colorings.

American alligators live in the swamps and lakes of the Coastal Plain region. Other common reptiles and amphibians found in North Carolina include southern leopard frogs, green anoles, skinks, bullfrogs, salamanders, red-spotted newts, snapping turtles, and eastern box turtles. There are 37 species of snakes. Most are harmless, including common corn snakes, garter snakes, and black racers. Venomous snakes include cottonmouths, copperheads, eastern diamondbacks, and timber rattlesnakes.

Black Racer

PLANTS AND ANIMALS

HISTORY

The first people to live in the North Carolina area arrived about 10,000 years ago. These Paleo-Indians were the ancestors of today's Native Americans. They were nomads who used stone spear points to hunt herds of large animals such as mastodons and bison. Other people eventually entered the area and built villages.

By the early 1500s, several Native American cultures had established themselves. They included the Catawba, Tuscarora, and Cherokee people.

A 1585 sketch of Pomeiooc, a Native American village near today's Gibbs Creek, North Carolina. Huts and longhouses sit inside a protective fence.

An English colony was established on Roanoke Island in 1587. When a supply ship arrived in 1590, no one was there. The name of a nearby island, "Croatoan," was found, but it was deserted, too. The settlement became known as "The Lost Colony."

The first European to visit North Carolina was Italian explorer Giovanni da Verrazzano, who worked for King Francis I of France. He arrived by ship in 1524 and briefly explored the Cape Fear area before moving on.

In 1540, Explorer Hernando de Soto and an expedition of 600 Spanish conquistadors passed through the western mountains. They unsuccessfully searched for gold.

In 1585, Sir Walter Raleigh of England sent settlers to Roanoke Island in the Outer Banks. They failed, and soon returned to England. More colonists arrived in 1587. When an English supply ship arrived three years later, all 118 colonists had vanished without a trace. Today, the settlement is known as "The Lost Colony."

North Carolina's first successful European settlement was established in 1650. They were colonists from neighboring Virginia. They built log homes near Albemarle Sound. By this time, the land had officially been named Carolina, in honor of England's King Charles I. By the 1680s, thousands of English colonists came to farm the land.

The European settlers took more and more land, angering the Tuscarora Native Americans. Starting in 1711, they fought a war with the colonists that lasted several years. The Native Americans suffered many deaths. Most of the survivors left North Carolina.

In 1710, to make governing the large colony easier, it was split into north and south. In 1729, North Carolina officially became a British crown colony. More settlers poured into the area.

Tuscarora Native Americans track European colonists in eastern North Carolina at the beginning of the Tuscarora War (1711-1715).

Harvesting cotton on a North Carolina plantation.

In 1776, North Carolina joined the other 12 American colonies in declaring independence from Great Britain. After the Revolutionary War (1775-1783), North Carolina became the 12th state when it ratified, or approved, the United States Constitution on November 21, 1789. The city of Raleigh became the state capital.

North Carolina depended heavily on agriculture. Large plantations grew tobacco and cotton. They depended on slave labor to make a bigger profit. Hundreds of thousands of African slaves were brought to North Carolina to do the backbreaking work of planting and harvesting crops.

In 1861, North Carolina joined the other slave-owning states of the Southern Confederacy and seceded, or left, the Union. It was the last state to join the Confederacy. During the Civil War (1861-1865), more than 100,000 North Carolinians fought against the North. However, many in the state disagreed with secession. Thousands fought for the Union. Most of the war's major battles occurred in other states. When the South lost the war in 1865, North Carolina's slaves were freed.

It took many years for North Carolina to rebuild its war-torn cities and farms. In the 1880s, the state worked to diversify its economy so that it wasn't so dependent on agriculture. Hydroelectric dams made cheap electricity that attracted new businesses and residents. The state's universities also helped North Carolina modernize. Its cities grew rapidly. By the 1920s, North Carolina's cotton mills made more fabric than anywhere else in the country. The state also was a big producer of furniture and tobacco products.

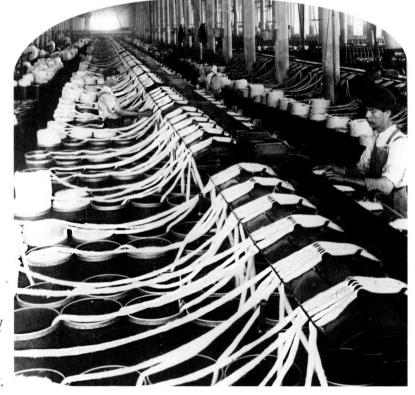

Workers make yarn in White Oak Mills, a busy cotton mill in Greensboro, North Carolina.

Racial strife from the Civil War festered for decades. "Jim Crow" laws forced African Americans to use separate schools and other facilities. Other laws kept many blacks from voting. The civil rights movement of the 1960s finally brought legal protection to African Americans and other minorities. Many wounds, however, have not yet fully healed.

A 16-year-old high school student from Monroe, North Carolina, at a civil rights protest in 1961.

As tobacco farming, textiles, and furniture making have declined in recent years, high-tech industries and banking have taken their place. North Carolina's top-rated universities help make the state a leader in scientific research. Today, North Carolina continues to grow and prosper.

DID YOU KNOW?

• Cape Hatteras Lighthouse is the tallest lighthouse in the United States. For decades, it warned sailors of the treacherous, underwater sandbars of the Diamond Shoals near Hatteras Island. The sandy island is part of the Outer Banks of North Carolina's Atlantic Ocean coast. The Outer Banks are nicknamed "The Graveyard of the Atlantic" because of the hundreds of shipwrecks that have occurred offshore. The lighthouse has distinctive white and black spiral stripes. It was completed in 1870. It stands 198 feet (60 m) tall, with 269 steps to the top. Its light can be seen more than 28 miles (45 km) away in clear weather. The historic lighthouse was recently moved farther inland to protect it from erosion caused by ocean waves.

• Blackbeard was one of the most feared and cunning pirates to ever sail the Spanish Main. In the early 1700s, he and his crew of cutthroats terrorized the Caribbean Sea and the eastern seaboard of North America. In 1718, he sailed to North Carolina, where he made his home for a time. In November 1718, Blackbeard was finally killed in a fierce battle with the British navy. The battle took place near Ocracoke Island in North Carolina's Outer Banks. Legends say that the pirate's headless body swam three times around his ship before finally sinking to Davy Jones' Locker (the bottom of the sea).

• On December 17, 1903, Wilbur and Orville Wright made the first controlled flights of a powered airplane. They flew at Big Kill Devil Hill, a large sand dune near the Outer Banks town of Kitty Hawk. Orville made the first flight. He piloted the *Wright Flyer* aircraft on a 12-second journey that covered just 120 feet (37 m).

DID YOU KNOW?

PEOPLE

Stephen Curry (1988-) is a point guard for the National Basketball Association's Golden State Warriors. Famed for his shooting skills, especially three-pointers, he was named the NBA's Most Valuable Player in 2015, after leading his team to victory in the NBA championship series. During the 2014-2015 season, he scored 118 points in the team's first three games, the first player to do so since fellow North Carolinian Michael Jordan in 1989-1990. Curry was born in Ohio, but he grew up in Charlotte, North Carolina.

Dale Earnhardt Jr. (1974-) is a NASCAR stock car racer. He has won the Daytona 500 twice, in 2004 and 2014. Fans have voted to honor him with NASCAR's Most Popular Driver Award 13 times. Earnhardt was born in Kannapolis, North Carolina. Many of his family members are also current or former race car drivers, including his father, the legendary Hall of Fame driver Dale Earnhardt Sr.

Andy Griffith (1926-2012) was an actor, singer, comedian, writer, and television producer. He starred in many films and television series. He is best known for his 1960s role as Sheriff Andy Taylor in *The Andy Griffith Show*. The series was set in fictional Mayberry, North Carolina. Griffith was partly inspired by Mount Airy, North Carolina, the small town where he was born and grew up.

Levi Coffin (1798-1877) was a businessman and teacher who helped thousands of slaves escape to freedom in the years before the Civil War (1861-1865). He used money from his businesses to buy food and clothing for people who ran Underground Railroad "stations." Despite the danger, he also ran a station in his own home, helping runaway slaves escape. After the war, he spent money to help feed, clothe, and educate former slaves. Coffin was born in Guilford County, North Carolina.

Dolley Madison (1768-1849) was the wife of James Madison, the fourth president of the United States. President Madison served from 1809 to 1817. As First Lady, Dolley Madison was known for being cheerful, and for being a gracious hostess. She also showed her bravery during the War of 1812. She helped rescue art and important papers from the White House in 1814 before British soldiers burned much of the city. Dolley Madison was born in Guilford County, North Carolina.

Earl Scruggs (1924-2012) was a master of the banjo, especially the three-finger picking style. He shot to fame in the 1940s when he played in Bill Monroe's bluegrass band, The Blue Grass Boys. In the 1950s and 1960s, he played with guitarist Lester Flatt in their own band, The Foggy Mountain Boys. Scruggs is also famous for playing "The Ballad of Jed Clampett" on the 1960s television show *The Beverly Hillbillies*. Scruggs was born in Cleveland County, North Carolina.

John Coltrane (1926-1967) was a jazz saxophonist, bandleader, and composer. His groundbreaking, experimental jazz performances have influenced generations of musicians. His most acclaimed album was 1965's *A Love Supreme*. Coltrane was inducted into the Jazz Hall of Fame in 1965. He won a Grammy Lifetime Achievement Award in 1992. In 1957, Coltrane recorded with legendary jazz pianist and fellow North Carolinian Thelonious Monk. Coltrane was born in Hamlet, North Carolina.

CITIES

Charlotte is the largest city in North Carolina. Its population is 809,958. It is located in the south-central part of the state's Piedmont region. Charlotte is a major banking and finance center. Some of the country's biggest banks have their headquarters in the city, including Bank of America and Wells Fargo Securities. Other top employers include health care, transportation, and retail. The University of North Carolina at Charlotte enrolls more than 28,000 students. The Mint Museum's two locations display hundreds of pieces of fine art from all over the world. The NASCAR Hall of Fame honors the nation's best drivers with racing artifacts, historic cars, videos, and racing simulators.

Capitol Building

Raleigh is the capital of North Carolina. It is also the second-largest city in the state. Its population is about 439,896. Founded in 1792, it is located in the east-central Piedmont region. The city is named after England's Sir Walter Raleigh, the nobleman who sponsored North Carolina's first settlements in the 1500s. Today, Raleigh is a center for banking, health care, and education. North Carolina State University enrolls more than 34,000 students. Duke University is in nearby Durham. Also in the area is the University of North Carolina at Chapel Hill. Together, the Raleigh-Durham-Chapel Hill metropolitan area has a population of more than 2 million people. The three cities anchor the Research Triangle, a region that is home to many high-tech companies and science research labs.

Greensboro is located in the north-central part of the Piedmont region. Its population is about 282,586. The city is near the site of 1781's Battle of Guilford Courthouse, a major clash in the Revolutionary War (1775-1783). The city is named after General Nathanael Greene, who led the Patriot army during the battle. Greensboro was once home to many textile mills, tobacco processors, and furniture-making companies. Today, the city's economy depends more on insurance, transportation, and high-technology companies. The International Civil Rights Center and Museum preserves the F.W. Woolworth building where four African American students refused to leave the "white's only" lunch counter in 1960. Their brave actions ignited national "sit-in" civil rights protests.

Winston-Salem is located in the northwest part of the Piedmont region. Its population is 239,269. It was two separate cities until 1913, when they merged. Long a center for tobacco, furniture making, and textiles, the city today relies more on banking, food processing, medical research, and electronic equipment manufacturing. Nationally acclaimed Wake Forest University enrolls more than 7,500 students. Winston-Salem is often called "The City of the Arts" because of its many galleries and workshops, and for its support of artist groups. Old Salem is a historic district in the city. It features living history exhibits—including blacksmiths, cobblers, and bakers—that explain life in 1700s and 1800s.

TRANSPORTATION

North Carolina has one of the biggest and best-maintained road systems in the United States. There are 106,202 miles (170,916 km) of public roadways in the state. A web of interstate and state highways connects major cities with the rest of the country.

There are 23 freight railroads that haul heavy cargo across North Carolina on 3,259 miles (5,245 km) of track. The most common goods carried include chemicals, stone, coal, lumber, and farm products. Passengers are whisked across North Carolina on six Amtrak rail lines.

The Hatteras/Ocracoke ferry is one of the most popular of the seven coastal routes. It runs multiple times per day, 365 days per year, transporting people and their vehicles to and from the Outer Banks.

North Carolina has 74 publicly owned airports and almost 300 privately owned airports. There are 9 major commercial airports. Charlotte-Douglas International Airport is one of the 10 busiest airports in the country. It handles nearly 45 million passengers each year. Raleigh-Durham International Airport handles about 10 million passengers.

North Carolina has two deepwater ports where large, oceangoing ships load the state's products and transport them to markets all over the world. They include the Port of Wilmington and the Port of Morehead City.

Each year, about 2 million passengers use ferry boats to reach the islands of the Outer Banks. Since 1934, the North Carolina Department of Transportation Ferry Division has run one of the biggest ferry systems in the country. More than 22 boats operate on 7 routes daily.

TRANSPORTATION

NATURAL
RESOURCES

A century ago, agriculture was the biggest industry in North Carolina. Today, agriculture is much smaller, although it is still important. There are about 48,800 farms in the state. Most of the farms are small, averaging just 170 acres (69 ha). The value of the state's yearly farm production is about $12.5 billion.

North Carolina's most valuable crops include tobacco, soybeans, corn, sweet potatoes, hay, wheat, and cotton. The state's farmers also grow peanuts, melons, apples, strawberries, bell peppers, cucumbers, cabbage, squash, and beans. North Carolina is also a top-ranked state for raising hogs and poultry.

North Carolina's commercial fleets catch many kinds of fish and shellfish in the Atlantic Ocean. The top fish species include menhaden, Atlantic croaker, and flounder. The top shellfish include blue crabs and shrimp.

Free-range pigs raised on a farm in Asheville, North Carolina.

About 60 percent of North Carolina is covered by forestland. Furniture making is a big part of the state's forest products industry, despite cheap overseas competition. The entire forest products industry employs more than 67,000 in the state.

About 300 kinds of minerals are found in North Carolina's mines. The state is a leading producer of feldspar, mica, and pyrophyllite. Other products mined in North Carolina include lithium, clay, quartz, and granite.

INDUSTRY

In recent years, foreign competition and economic downturns have caused North Carolina's textile, agriculture, and furniture industries to fade. In their place, the state now attracts medical research laboratories, electronics and computer manufacturers, plus banking and finance companies.

The Research Triangle—the area between the cities of Raleigh, Durham, and Chapel Hill—has boomed in recent years with the rise of new high-tech manufacturers. The state's other chief manufactured goods include transportation equipment, plastics, chemicals, tobacco products, medicines, processed foods, household furniture, plus fabric and clothing.

The service industry represents a large part of the state's economy. Instead of manufacturing products, service industries sell services to businesses and consumers. It includes businesses such as advertising, banking, financial services, health care, insurance, restaurants, retail stores, law, marketing, and tourism.

An employee of the Hickory Chair Furniture Company examines the work being done on a chair. The North Carolina company has been in business since 1911.

A scene from the television show Sleepy Hollow *is filmed on a street in downtown Wilmington, North Carolina.*

Hundreds of major films and television shows have been produced in North Carolina, thanks to generous tax breaks. A few of the productions recently shot in the state include *Iron Man 3*, *Under the Dome*, and *Sleepy Hollow*.

Tourism plays a big part of the state's economy. Millions of visitors travel to North Carolina each year to enjoy its scenic beauty, history, and Southern culture. Travelers spend more than $21 billion yearly, which supports nearly 205,000 jobs.

SPORTS

North Carolina has three major league sports teams. The Carolina Panthers play in the National Football League (NFL). They have won several division championships and have appeared in the Super Bowl twice. The team plays at Bank of America Stadium in Charlotte.

The Charlotte Hornets compete in the Southeast Division of the National Basketball Association (NBA). In 2010, the team was bought by basketball legend and North Carolina native Michael Jordan.

The Carolina Hurricanes play in the National Hockey League (NHL). Based in Raleigh, the team won the Stanley Cup championship for the 2005-2006 season.

College sports are very popular in North Carolina. Basketball is especially big. Four North Carolina university teams consistently rank among the best in the nation. They include the Duke University Blue Devils in Durham, the Tar Heels of the University of North Carolina at Chapel Hill, the North Carolina State University Wolfpack in Raleigh, and the Wake Forest University Demon Deacons in Winston-Salem.

A NASCAR auto race at Charlotte Motor Speedway in Concord, North Carolina.

Auto racing is a huge spectator event for many North Carolinians. Stock car racing is the official state sport. There are many tracks that host NASCAR races. The biggest is Charlotte Motor Speedway, which holds 94,000 fans. Most of NASCAR's racing teams are based in North Carolina.

SPORTS

ENTERTAINMENT

A popular beach on North Carolina's Outer Banks.

North Carolina is filled with parks and historic sites. The Wright Brothers National Memorial is in Kill Devil Hills, on the Outer Banks. It marks the spot where Orville and Wilbur Wright made the first powered flight. Farther south is Cape Hatteras, a protruding section of the Outer Banks. The pristine, sandy beaches are protected by Cape Hatteras National Seashore.

The Fort Raleigh National Historic Site on Roanoke Island protects portions of the first English settlement in America. Also on the island is one of the state's three North Carolina Aquarium sites. Visitors can see sharks, stingrays, sea turtles, and many other kinds of aquatic life. The other two aquariums are at Fort Fisher and Pine Knoll Shores.

Tourists visit the 315-foot (96-m) Chimney Rock. It overlooks Hickory Nut Gorge and Lake Lure in the Blue Ridge Mountains area of western North Carolina.

The North Carolina Symphony plays most of its concerts in Raleigh's Meymandi Concert Hall. Founded in 1932, it tours all over North Carolina. It plays many free concerts for students.

Great Smoky Mountains National Park is in the Blue Ridge Mountains of western North Carolina. Shared by neighboring Tennessee, it is the most-visited park in the United States. More than 9.4 million people witness the park's breathtaking mountain views each year.

TIMELINE

8000 BC—The first Paleo-Indians venture into the North Carolina area.

1500s—Catawba, Tuscarora, and Cherokee Native Americans settle in the North Carolina area.

1524—Italian explorer Giovanni da Verrazzano is the first European to explore parts of present-day North Carolina.

1540—Spanish explorer Hernando de Soto passes through the western mountains of present-day North Carolina.

1585 and 1587—Sir Walter Raleigh sends English settlers to start a colony on Roanoke Island. Both attempts fail.

1650—Colonists from Virginia start the first successful settlement in North Carolina.

1715—Native Americans lose the four-year Tuscarora War against white settlers.

1776—North Carolina is first of the 13 American colonies to demand freedom from British rule.

1789—North Carolina becomes the 12th state in the Union.

1861—Civil War starts. North Carolina joins the rebel Confederate States of America.

1903—First powered airplane flight near the town of Kitty Hawk, North Carolina.

1960—Four African American students refuse to leave a "white's only" lunch counter. Their "sit-in" sparked a civil rights movement that helped stop Jim Crow laws, forcing African Americans to use separate facilities.

1970s—Modernization of North Carolina's economy begins with a shift toward technology and science research.

2006—The Carolina Hurricanes win the National Hockey League's Stanley Cup.

2015—The Duke University Blue Devils win the NCAA Men's Basketball Championship.

GLOSSARY

Barrier Islands

Long and narrow landforms just offshore from a mainland. Typically these islands are made up of sand, silt, or pebbles.

Civil Rights Movement

A nationwide effort beginning in the 1950s to reform federal and state laws so that African Americans and other minorities could enjoy full equality with whites.

Civil War

The war fought between America's Northern and Southern states from 1861-1865. The Southern states were for slavery. They wanted to start their own country. Northern states fought against slavery and a division of the country.

Colony

A group of people who settle in a distant territory but remain citizens of their native country.

Jim Crow Laws

Laws enacted to discriminate against African American people, such as forcing people of color to use separate drinking fountains, restaurants, and bathrooms from those used by white people. Other Jim Crow laws made it difficult for African Americans to vote. Jim Crow was the name of a character in a 19th-century plantation song in America's Southern states.

NASCAR

The National Association for Stock Car Auto Racing. Formed in 1948, NASCAR oversees the largest and most popular racing series in the world, including the Sprint Cup Series, the Xfinity Series, and the Camping World Truck Series.

Outer Banks

A long string of barrier islands that extends for about 200 miles (322 km) along the eastern coast of North Carolina. These sandy islands help to protect North Carolina's coastline from the rough seas of the Atlantic Ocean.

Piedmont

An Italian word that means "at the foot of the mountains."

Plateau

A large area of land that is mainly flat but much higher than the land surrounding it.

Revolutionary War

The war fought between the American colonies and Great Britain from 1775-1783. It is also known as the American Revolution, or the War of Independence.

Spanish Main

Spain's colonial territories in North and South America in the 1500s and 1600s. The term most often refers to Spain's colonies along the north coast of South America, Mexico, and the islands of the Caribbean Sea and the Gulf of Mexico.

Underground Railroad

In the early- to mid-1800s, people created the Underground Railroad to help African Americans escape from slave states. Not an actual railroad, it was instead a secret network of safe houses and connecting routes that led slaves to freedom.

INDEX